Employment Screening Business Secrets

How to Get More Clients, Keep Them Longer &
Quit Selling on Low Price

Mason Duchatschek

Jessica Coffey

Tyler Weston

Disclaimer

The Publisher and the Authors make no representations or warranties in any form or by any means with respect to the accuracy or completeness of the contents of this work and specifically disclaim all warranties, including (without limitation) warranties of fitness for a particular purpose. No warranty may be created or extended by sales or promotional materials. The advice and strategies contained herein may not be suitable for every situation, person, nonprofit organization, or business. This work is sold with the understanding that the Publisher is not engaged in rendering legal, accounting, or other related professional services. If professional assistance is required, the services of a competent professional person should be sought. Neither the Publisher nor the Authors shall be liable for damages arising therefrom. The fact that an organization or website is referred to in this work as a citation and/or a potential source of further information does not mean that the Authors or the Publisher endorses the information the organization or website may provide or recommendations it may make. In some, but not all, cases, affiliate income may be generated to the Authors from products or services purchased by readers from sites that are referred to in this work. Further, readers should be aware that internet websites listed in this work may have changed or disappeared between when this work was written and when it is read.

CONTENTS

Introduction

I f you are looking for an unfair advantage for your background check and employment screening business, as well as newer and better ways of getting more customers and earning more profit from each of them, then you're in the right place.

Our goal is to help you get the freedom to do what you do best and like to do most, so you can have a solid business, running your way … a business you can do anything you want with.

We also want to help you get the most out of every dollar you invest in your business without putting an unnecessary strain on your resources.

If you feel the secrets we're about to share with you make sense, then we suspect you will have questions at some point and will want to know the simple step-by-step pathway that turns the secrets we're going to share with you into action.

Here's some additional good news: We have added a workbook that will guide you along a simple path, and most of the time-consuming "grunt work" associated with creating marketing content has been done for you!

If you decide this advice isn't for you, at least you won't be caught off guard as the improvements we plan to bring to the background check industry in the very near future take hold. At the very least, you will learn about what's coming and how it will impact your industry so you can be prepared for it.

If what you read makes sense and you want to know more about how your background check and employment screening company can become a strategic partner—and get help executing the ideas mentioned in this book, along with wholesale pricing, product support, and additional training on the products mentioned in this book—simply click on the link labeled "How to Become a Strategic Partner" at https://amo-humancapital.com/ *and answer the questions on the short questionnaire that is presented. We will follow up with you once your information has been reviewed.*

Chapter 1

The Starting Point

We recently surveyed leaders in the background check industry and received results indicating an interest in retaining customers, growing the business without having to sell, and earning more profit. As a result, we have compiled a "how to" book and workbook with step-by-step details. It couldn't be easier unless we came and did it for you, and that would cost thousands of dollars a day.

We promise that you are going to learn our best strategies on how to build a force field around your existing client base, get new account referrals without having to ask, and generate additional revenue at higher profit margins with little or no extra effort—even if you or your staff hate to sell or aren't very good at it. Fair enough?

The first thing we want to mention is that if you've lost important clients, had existing clients try to nickel-and-dime you, or noticed it is harder than ever to get in front of new prospects when they're ready to buy, it's not your fault.

There's a lot of information out there and it can be confusing. Many times, that information overload keeps you from success. It's OK.

If you've been concerned in the past that you just can't succeed if you make even subtle changes to the way you've always done things, we're here to put those fears to rest. You can do this. You just need the right people to explain it to you.

There are a lot of good reasons to be in the background check and employment screening business. Every company that hires people needs background check services. That's a lot of prospects—and that's a good thing!

Plus, once you have an account, it's a residual income stream that pays you every time there's a job opening regardless of whether it's from growth, retirements, or regular turnover. We get it.

But what happens when a bigger competitor—or even a smaller but more desperate competitor—comes along and undercuts you? Loyalty isn't what it used to be, is it?

As much as we hate to admit it, clients and prospects tend to view background check services as a commodity. They want it fast. They want it right. They want it cheap.

There are lots of people who can meet those demands, and it sucks when you find yourself competing against all those other service providers who are willing to keep cutting prices to get new accounts or keep their existing accounts. You know the type.

Want to know how to change that game so it doesn't have to be such a dog-eat-dog industry?

THAT, friend, is EXACTLY what we will walk you through—step by step. We have the answers, and we'll share them with you. It's a win-win scenario for all involved. We're talking about you, us, and all our clients. You'll see.

We're going to walk you through strategies, tools, and tactics that will help you add more of your ideal clients, increase profit from your existing client base with little or no extra effort, and find out how to outmaneuver and outsmart your rivals before they even realize what happened.

Have you ever noticed how competitive the fast-food industry is? There are so many choices and options. Everywhere you look it seems like there are "dollar menus" and restaurants undercutting each other on price just to get people in the door.

If you're like us, you've probably wondered how anybody can make money selling burgers for a dollar. These companies spend big money on advertising to sell burgers, for example, for next to nothing, and yet more and more fast-food restaurants are doing it. Companies like McDonalds, Burger King, and Hardees have to practically give away their burgers at rock-bottom prices just to respond to market forces and remain competitive.

It sounds kind of like the background check business sometimes, doesn't it? Prospects and clients expect better deals or they will go elsewhere. Clients and prospects expect you to practically give away your services or they will find someone else who will.

To someone who is hungry, a burger from McDonalds, Burger King, or Hardees can do the job. And to a company needing background checks, there are lots of different companies who can do those jobs as well.

The big secret is that these restaurants don't just offer burgers. Items like the soft drinks that go along with the burgers bring MUCH higher profit margins—which industry experts claim are around 90%! By adding high-profit-margin products (soft drinks, etc.) that complement their core offering (burgers), these restaurant owners experience prosperity instead of poverty.

We think one of the solutions to growing your business has to do with YOU offering high-profit-margin products and services that complement your core offerings as well. Ideally, those complementary, high-profit-margin products should not be a commodity (like a background check) that people can go get anywhere for a cheaper price. Ideally, they should also sell themselves, with little or no effort or marketing expense.

It just so happens we have products your prospects and clients need, and we offer wholesale pricing (along with great margins) to the background check companies we agree to work with. In the spirit of full disclosure, if what you are about to read makes sense, we are going to want to talk to you, and we invite you to reach out if you have any questions. The background check companies we elect to work with get wholesale pricing on our products, as well as access to "done-for-you" marketing materials and templates, client training videos, and customer support.

Here's the backstory. Mason was in his early 20s when he took his first outside sales job. He was selling tickets for sales training seminars to automotive dealerships in midwestern markets for a very talented, but little-known, up-and-coming sales trainer.

He made decent money and learned a lot, but when he looks back on it, other than the experience and people he met, it was rough. And that might be an understatement.

He would arrive in a market about 8 weeks before the seminar was supposed to take place, open the yellow pages in the phone book, and write down the phone number of every auto dealership within a 60-mile radius. For those prospects he was able to get in front of, he was giving a memorized presentation, answering objections, and asking for the order. It was old-school selling at its worst. And make no mistake, as a young 22-year-old selling sales training to general managers of car dealerships who almost ALL thought they were God's gift to the automotive sales industry, it was brutal.

When people say they don't like to make cold calls or push products or services—even if they're good products or services—we understand completely! It sucked, and he swore he would NEVER do anything like that again.

The worst part was that after he worked one market, he had to pick up and go do it again in another market starting from scratch. It was a one-time sale. There was no residual income. There was no way to build upon any relationships and trust in a market he had previously served, other than that some of the attendees were willing to serve as references to dealers in other markets.

Even though the pay was great, it was a REALLY tough way to make a living, and at a certain point the money didn't matter. It was a rough road. He had to find a better way. The good news is that he did, and we're about to share it with you.

Jes, on the other hand, spent years in the human resources and recruiting field. She worked with start-up companies as well as various large corporations. The main focus of her job was spending time working with corporate leaders to reduce employee turnover, increase employee engagement, and help the organizations she worked for get the right people in the right jobs.

She experienced firsthand the joys associated with hiring right the first time. She experienced the headaches, hassles, and expenses related to mistakes in hiring. She saw the financial consequences of inefficiency, complacency, and disengaged employees.

One day Mason read an article featuring an interview with Fred Smith, the founder of FedEx. Fred said he used to go to parties and listen to what people complained about, and he encouraged aspiring entrepreneurs to do the same—and start a business if they could figure out a way to fix what people were complaining about.

And you know what Mason heard general managers of auto dealerships complaining about? They complained about the high turnover of salespeople. In fact, that was one of the objections he heard frequently, which he halfway bought into. Some general managers had such high turnover that they hesitated to invest in training new reps; they had very little confidence the reps would stay long enough for them to recoup the investment made in training them.

General managers told Mason they had used traditional methods and hired good reps. They also admitted that they had used those exact same methods to hire people they wished they hadn't. They expressed frustration because they realized their traditional methods couldn't help them predict, with any degree of certainty, the likelihood that a job applicant was likely to succeed.

The general managers went on to complain about the shortcomings of traditional methods. For example, they knew their hiring decisions were only as sound as the facts on which they were based. But so many applicants lied or embellished on their applications and resumes that they couldn't tell fact from fiction.

They talked about how applicants wouldn't give out names of people as references who would say anything bad about them. They complained that drug tests only proved someone could stay clean for 30 days, and criminal background checks only showed when someone was caught and successfully prosecuted. Criminal background checks were completely incapable of showing who was caught doing things they weren't supposed to be doing if they weren't prosecuted, or they weren't prosecuted successfully—even if they were guilty.

One day, Mason came across an article in *Personal Selling Power* magazine that featured a study by Michigan State University's School of Business on predicting success in the workplace. It said pre-employment testing was the #1 predictor of future success by a 3-to-1 margin over interviews, past experience, and education.

Mason felt like he had discovered a set of unmet needs. So he decided to take Fred Smith of FedEx's advice.

Mason started researching industrial psychologists across the country and the assessment tools they created for pre-employment assessment purposes, as well as employee development and engagement. And he came across an industrial psychologist by the name of Neal Johnston. He felt Neal's work was exceptional, so he bought the marketing rights to his products and went into business selling them.

Mason's hunch paid off, and he found the pre-employment assessments incredibly easy to sell. All he had to do was get a prospect to try one. His credibility went through the roof because prospects were amazed by the accuracy of the assessments and how well the reports described them.

Because hiring decisions either solved business problems or created new ones, employers wanted this kind of information on job applicants before they hired them. And sales managers, operations managers, and human resources directors now loved him because he was an ally who could help them identify, retain, and develop the best people. They no longer had to waste their time and resources on people who weren't a good fit.

Mason's mom always said that if you don't think you have the time to do something right the first time, it's even harder to find the time to do it over. It's been Mason's experience that when it comes to hiring, smart business owners and executives also know this to be true. Business owners and executives recognize that the investment in his assessment products is a fraction of the cost of a single hiring mistake, much less a bunch of them, so price isn't usually an objection.

Once assessments became part of his clients' selection process, Mason created a residual revenue stream selling assessment tools just like you have for background checks—only the profit margins were and still are WAY better. And because the assessments were unique, they weren't viewed as a commodity and rivals couldn't just undercut him on the same product, as they're probably doing to you right now with background checks.

The usefulness of the assessments went beyond pre-employment testing, too. Decision makers wanted this kind of information to pinpoint opportunities for growth and improved engagement within their existing ranks as well.

Want to learn how to get wholesale pricing on the same exact assessment tools Mason used to build his business? Want access to a "done-for-you" workbook that helps you use the ready-made marketing videos and other promotional content as if you created it yourself? Wouldn't it be nice to have an automated way to do most, if not all, of your selling, client training, and customer service without having to take away from your existing business? <u>It has all been done for you, and we are going to give it to you</u>.

To support the background check companies we want to work with, our videos are like a virtual sales and customer service department that sells and services clients for you, perfectly—24 hours a day, 365 days a year—and reaches an unlimited amount of prospects and clients simultaneously, worldwide. Because the videos are internet based, little or no effort, expense, or time is required to make that happen either.

Let that sink in. Read that one more time.

We know there are distractions everywhere. But the strategies we're about to share can change your life. We don't want you to miss a single crucial step.

For over 20 years, Mason has worked with and helped small mom-and-pop shops, as well as multibillion-dollar worldwide corporations, solve their common people-related business problems. Specifically, he has helped them reduce employee turnover, maximize employee engagement, reduce labor costs, reduce workers' comp costs, reduce shrinkage, and increase sales.

In your background check business, we suspect you've got some challenges similar to the ones we've faced, like finding consistent ways to get in front of your ideal prospects when they are ready to buy and finding ways to provide such exceptional value, that's so greatly in excess of what your competitors can offer, that current and potential clients can't even imagine doing business with anyone else.

It took Mason years of hard work and hundreds of thousands of dollars to figure all this out through trial and error, but we don't want it to be that way for you. Imagine what your life will be like after you learn how to earn referrals without even having to ask. Imagine opening your email or checking your voice mail to find messages from high-profile people and prominent companies you've never worked with before, asking if you can do some of the same remarkable things for them that you've already done for others.

Can you imagine how good it would feel to not have to worry about losing clients, wasting money on advertising, or having to go sell? Can you imagine what it would look like to see the upward arrow on your revenue charts when you look at your own financials, knowing that it took little or no extra effort to accomplish those revenue improvements? How much better would that make things for you?

We figured this out so you don't have to. If you can follow the simple step-by-step instructions that we have laid out for you and utilize the "done-for-you" marketing resources we've provided and position yourself correctly, you can grow your business quickly.

Chapter 2

Three Secrets and One Purple Cow

We want to share three secrets with YOU that your COMPETITORS will wish we didn't, especially if you APPLY the knowledge we're about to share, regardless of whether or not we ever speak, meet, or do business together. At the very least, we want you to be glad you invested your time with us, and hopefully you think of these little secrets as a gift from us to you.

Secret #1: Some people think the best way to keep your customers is to do a good job for a fair price. The real secret to client retention is to proactively prove that you are attentive to their needs and capable of finding new ways to save your clients far more than they spend on your services.

Clearly, some people believe that all they need to do to keep their clients is do a good job for a fair price. Well, if they're lucky, it may be enough in some cases. However, luck isn't a strategy.

Mason has a client whom he likes, respects, and trusts who was the CEO of a privately held Inc. 100 company, and she referred him to her new CPA. Here's why. She told him that this new CPA had found a little-known way to help another company like hers save hundreds of thousands of dollars PER YEAR in specific tax breaks and credits. She reached out to him and asked if he could help her company do the same and how much it would cost. He got back to her and the answer was yes, and it would only cost $1,000–$2,000, total. Working together would save her business hundreds of thousands of dollars PER YEAR.

If her old CPA firm didn't know how to capture the same savings, it was certainly a black eye on their professional reputation. If her old CPA DID know how and didn't bother to let her know, that was an even BIGGER black eye because it only proved they weren't paying attention to her company's needs and her company wasn't a priority. The CEO of that Inc. 100 company switched ALL her company's accounting business, which was A LOT, to this new CPA and his firm.

Did her old CPA firm successfully complete her company's tax returns for a fair price in years past? Yes, of course they did. Tax returns are largely viewed as a commodity service because any decent CPA firm can do them, and there are A LOT of CPA firms. In fact, accounting has become such a price-competitive commodity/service that you can now get your taxes done for you at Walmart.

Accounting firms are everywhere. But was doing quality tax returns enough to keep her business? No. A different CPA found multiple ways to save her company far more per year, in real dollars, than her company had spent for accounting services with her old CPA firm in the past. If you ask her—which we have—she will tell you that her NEW CPA firm is proactive, attentive, and always looking for revenue-generating and cost-saving opportunities.

Her new CPA firm proved with their deeds, rather than hollow promises, that she and her company are a priority. Whatever they charge in fees is a fraction of the cost of NOT doing business with them. Her new CPA firm is saving her more than her company spends for accounting services, which makes it BETTER than free.

Takeaway: The *first secret* to client retention is to make fees irrelevant by finding new ways to save clients far more than they spend on your services.

Secret #2: For many salespeople, converting a pro-spect into a customer without coming off like the un-pleasant stereotypes associated with salespeople is hard enough. However, the bigger challenge facing most background check companies is the double task of being positioned as THE subject matter expert AND getting in front of ideal prospects when those pro-spects are ready to buy. Some people think that to land more of your ideal high-profile, and most profit-able accounts, you need to be a good networker, mar-keter, advertiser, and salesperson—or you must hire other people who are. Want to know the truth?

The real *secret (#2)* to landing more of your ideal and most profitable clients is that it's much easier, faster, and less expensive if you can figure out a way to turn your existing clients into advocates and cheerleaders who do all that work FOR you for FREE, without you having to ask.

So yes, it helps when you can save them more than they spend with you, but you must ALSO proactively PROVE that you are attentive to your client's needs. They need to know you are always paying attention to their business and looking after their best interests as if they were your own.

Do the CPAs at Mason's client's new firm have to go to networking events, spend big bucks on advertising, hire sales reps, or try to do the selling themselves? The answer is NO. Do they have to spend all kinds of dollars on vanity ads trying to tell their marketplace how great they are? NO, because the RESULTS THEY DELIVER speak for themselves, prove their expertise, and solidify their position as trusted advisors and subject matter experts.

The cool thing is that their ideal prospects call THEM when they're ready for better results, and almost all those prospects ask some variation of the same question: Can you do for me what you did for the other client who referred me to you?

Guess what else? The CEO who switched CPA firms is just one of MANY who have become advocates and cheerleaders for her new CPA firm. She's not the only one paying it forward and telling others in her inner circle about them. Her new CPA firm is in the unique position of sorting through ideal prospects who want to become clients—rather than trying to convince cold leads to inquire about becoming clients.

One of the best ways to do that is to establish your expert status based on the RESULTS you deliver and DEMONSTRATE proactive attention to your clients' needs while PROVING UNIQUE VALUE and expertise clients don't feel they can get anywhere else.

Takeaway: The *second secret* to landing more of your ideal clients without having to market, sell, or even ask for referrals is to figure out a way to turn your existing clients into your advocates and cheerleaders who do all that work for you for free, without you having to ask.

It's important to remember that you must *do something exceptional, remarkable, and unique*. It's not enough to do a good job at what others say they can do too.

Secret #3: Some people think the best way to grow your profit is to get more clients. However, an often overlooked secret to growing your firm's revenue—and, more importantly, PROFIT—lies in finding ways to generate additional revenue streams that complement your existing services without interfering with what you currently offer or requiring many, if any, additional man-hours to deliver. As we mentioned earlier, think of it kind of like a hamburger stand deciding to offer fries and a shake with each burger they sell.

We're going to let you in on a little gem. Mason's dad once told him that people don't go to the hardware store because they need a drill. They go to the hardware store because they need a hole. Think about that.

Your clients don't come to you because they need background checks. Our clients don't come to us because they need employment tests. Our clients, meaning your clients and our clients, come to us because they need to reduce their risk of hiring mistakes and maximize the probability of hiring the best people. When it comes to hiring, employers who fail to get all the job-related information they can legally gather about applicants before making an offer are playing Russian roulette without checking all the chambers of the weapon first.

You're in the risk reduction business, and so are we. However, we aren't competitors, and we think we may be able to be allies. It's all about getting more clients, keeping them longer, getting paid more, and earning more referrals. When you discover how to add scalable revenue components to your business, your revenue increases but the work and man hours required to gain that additional revenue don't.

Takeaway: The *third little secret* we shared to landing more of your ideal clients without have to market, sell, or even ask for referrals is to identify unmet client and prospect needs in areas closely related to your existing expertise and services and fill those unmet needs.

The obvious question is, how do you build your business in a way that is congruent with the secrets we just shared with you? Well, we have the answer, and we're going to share it with you. Want a hint? It isn't doing more of what you've already been doing.

As we mentioned earlier, it's not enough to be great at what you do anymore—certainly not in a field like background checks, where there are so many other options for current and potential clients to choose from that all look about the same to the untrained eye.

How can you differentiate? Consider this.

Have you ever heard the term "Purple Cow"? Yes, we said PURPLE Cow. It's a term coined by Seth Godin, who wrote a book with the very same title. In his book, Godin described how he once found himself in a rural area in another part of the world, and as he was traveling, he noticed a brown cow by itself in a field. He described how it caught his attention as it grazed. The sun was reflecting off the dew in the grass, making it look like diamonds in the sunlight. But after a short time traveling the countryside, he had seen so many brown cows that he no longer found a brown cow interesting and thought they all looked the same. In fact, he said brown cows were boring.

Now, can you imagine what would happen if you drove just outside of town and saw a purple cow grazing by the side of the road—something you had never seen before, a totally unique and remarkable creature? If that happened outside any of our towns, there would be a line of cars parked to look at it, take pictures of it, and shoot video. It would be all over social media, and TV helicopters would be hovering overhead in no time flat.

Let's face it: As Godin says, the business world is full of brown cows. Brown cows are boring products and services we can get anywhere. It takes a ton of time and lots of money to convince even one person, much less a bunch of them, that one brown cow is any better than another brown cow. What companies have the unlimited amount of time necessary to convince all their prospects they are different? Who has that much money?

On the other hand, a Purple Cow is a unique and remarkable business or way of doing business that is so extraordinary that it's worth talking about, promoting, and sharing with anyone and everyone willing to listen. It's in a class by itself and is so phenomenal and exciting that people can't help but talk about it, and the story of its mere existence travels everywhere without effort or expense.

It's safe to say that most people look at background check companies like brown cows, but it doesn't have to be that way for your firm after today. Is there a way to transform your background check business into a Purple Cow? We think so. And we think doing so should be a HUGE part of your growth and/or profita-bility strategy. It is certainly part of ours.

If you're performing background checks, you know who is hiring and how much of it they're doing. If a company or industry you serve has lots of turnover, you know it. This gives you a HUGE advantage, strate-gically speaking, if you know what to do next.

Because turnover is expensive, at some point sooner or later your clients will decide to do something about it. If you can't or don't choose to be part of the solu-tion, they will find someone else who can and will give them the help they need.

Chapter 3

The Numbers Tell the Story

In Jim Collins's best-selling book *Good to Great*, he said the most important thing any business can do is get the right people on the bus and get the wrong people off the bus. More importantly, he said it is critical to get the right people in the right seats on the bus. The bus, of course, is their business.

Collins published his book in 2001, and people are still talking about it in seminars and boardrooms all over the world. Why? It's because he was right, and everyone knows it. What people who read his book DON'T know is HOW TO DO IT and WHAT TOOLS ARE NEEDED, because his book DIDN'T give those secrets away.

The second half of the book *People Matter Most* on Amazon.com DOES give away those secrets. It says EXACTLY how to do it—and even reveals the tools that are necessary. We know this because Mason WROTE that book. But you don't have to spend the money to buy that book or invest the time to read it, because we're going to tell you exactly what you need to know here. (Bonus: There is a link in Section 2 of Chapter 7 of this book where you can download the PDF of *People Matter Most* for FREE.)

How critical is it for a company to get the right people on their bus and into the right seats? Specifically, in terms of dollars and cents, how big of a deal is it? How much can an organization save if they do it well? And how much will the organization suffer if they don't?

Now, there's an easy way to find out, and here it is: Basically, we enter information clients should know off the top of their head, or be able to access easily, into our proprietary Human Capital Calculator. It's important to use a client's REAL numbers so THEY know the REAL rewards that are tied to their strategic decisions and tactical courses of action.

Tier 1 W2 Count ❶	Tier 1 Employee Count ❶	Tier 1 Annual Salary ❶
35	25	50000

Tier 1 Turnover Expense Rate ★ 21% ❶	Tier 1 Turnover Reduction Percent ★ 25% ❶

Tier 1 Turnover Cost ❶	Tier 1 Turnover Savings ❶
105000.00	26250.00

Tier 2 - For positions paying less than $30,000/yr

Tier 2 W2 Count	Tier 2 Employee Count	Tier 2 Annual Salary
300	120	25000

Tier 2 Turnover Expense Rate ★ 16% ❶	Tier 2 Turnover Reduction Percent ★ 25%

Tier 2 Turnover Cost	Tier 2 Turnover Savings
720000.00	180000.00

Tier 3 - For executives and physicians

Tier 3 W2 Count	Tier 3 Employee Count	Tier 3 Annual Salary
6	5	150000

Tier 3 Turnover Expense Rate: 1.82% ❶	Tier 3 Turnover Reduction Percent ★ 25%

Tier 3 Turnover Cost	Tier 3 Turnover Savings
	68250.00

ltalcalculator.com/Value-Calculator/Worksheet/WID/57#top

Once the data is entered, the Human Capital Calculator will provide a custom report showcasing real costs—as well as potential savings tied to improvements—associated with employee turnover and employee engagement. The longer version of the report can also address issues related to workers' compensation, shrinkage/employee theft, client retention, and new account acquisition. Let's take a quick look at how to evaluate the details of the report related to EM-PLOYEE TURNOVER.

How much does it cost a company, specifically, when they put the wrong people in the wrong positions and the employees leave? This tool (which we make available to our strategic partners in the background check industry) will help determine the dollar cost of employee turnover and calculate the financial rewards that are tied to achieving targeted and measurable improvement goals.

We simply plug in things like how many people a prospect or client lost, how many they have left, and their average salaries, and the Human Capital Calculator report will tell us how much it costs that prospect or client each time they lose a person, as well as the total the cost of losing all the people they lost for the year. It will even calculate the potential savings they could recover based on their ability to achieve their goals for reducing turnover.

For example, here's how it works using data we plugged into the calculator for a sample manufacturing company with 150 employees and a payroll of $5.5 million, not including overtime costs. As shown below, there are three tiers or categories of employees.

(# of w2's) - (# of employees)	* Avg. Annual Salary	* Turnover Expense Rate	Total
35 - 25	X $50,000	* 21%	$105,000

Tier 2 - For positions paying less than $30,000/yr

(# of w2's) - (# of employees)	* Avg. Annual Salary	* Turnover Expense Rate	Total
300 - 120	X $25,000	* 16%	$720,000

Tier 3 - For executives and physicians

(# of w2's) - (# of employees)	* Avg. Annual Salary	* Turnover Expense Rate	Total
6 - 5	X $150,000	* 182%	$273,000

Total Turnover Cost = $1,098,000

Total Turnover Savings = $274,500

STRATEGIES

1. Improve 'Job Match' when hiring (skill, attitude, behavior)
2. Improve retention (minimize conflict and drama)

Tier 1 is composed of all the people who are not executives or physicians but are earning more than $30,000 a year as technicians, salespeople, managers, and other professionals. According to various researchers, it costs approximately 21% of their average salary to replace each person lost in these roles. That's what we call the turnover expense rate.

Tier 2 is composed of hourly and production employees typically making less than $30,000 a year. According to various researchers, it costs about 16% of their average salary to replace each person lost in these positions.

Tier 3 is composed of executives and/or physicians, and various researchers estimate that the cost to replace each one of these people who is lost ranges from 150% to 213% of their average annual salary. In this example, we picked a turnover expense rate right in the middle at 182%.

Of course, if a client has done internal turnover cost studies, the calculator will allow us to plug in their own custom turnover expense rate for each of these tiers of employees. To calculate the cost of turnover for each of these tiers, the calculator simply subtracts the number of current employees from the number of W-2s produced last year, and then multiplies that number by the average salary for people in that tier. Finally, the remaining number is multiplied by the turnover expense rate for people in each of the tiers to calculate the cost of turnover for that tier.

When we add up the total cost of turnover for each of the tiers, then we know how much employee turnover costs that business each year. In this example, the total cost of turnover is $1,098,000. Since we plugged in a goal of achieving a 25% reduction in turnover, the report indicates a potential savings of $274,500 per year if they can pull that off—and more if that company can do better! (That adds up to $2,745,000 over 10 years if there is a way to reduce turnover by something as meager as 25% and maintain those improvements.)

Below the data, you'll see some of the suggested strategies and tactics for helping that company achieve their targeted turnover reduction goals.

Strategy number 1 is improving the job match by making sure people have the skills, attitude, and personality required by the job. People don't want to stay in positions that rub them the wrong way and cause friction.

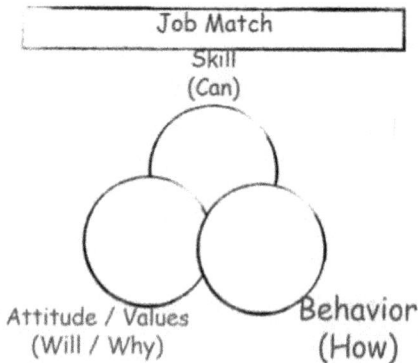

As our friend and colleague Hank Epstein, a consultant from Washington, Missouri, often says, "Everyone has two jobs. The first job is doing what their boss expects, and the other is protecting their job."

Employees want to look good, and it's hard when they are in a role that requires them to act like or pretend to be something they aren't.

Strategy number 2 is to improve retention by minimizing unnecessary conflict and drama at work, particularly between individuals and their supervisors, where they often feel most powerless and frustrated. Matching people to the right supervisors can be a highly effective retention strategy as well.

```
┌─────────────────────────────────┐
│       Leadership Match          │
└─────────────────────────────────┘
```

Team
Leader

↓

Team Member

If we examine the Human Capital Calculator report summary, it's all there for you—and more importantly, for your clients—to see. Underneath the $274,500 ANNUAL savings they get if they can reduce turnover by 25%, it shows the number of employees and W-2s, the annual turnover costs, and the target amount they selected for improvement, in this case 25%.

Use of this section of the tool demonstrates the importance of hiring and keeping the right people in the right positions and eliminating the kind of drama and conflict that drives them away or makes them disengaged and unproductive.

Can you see how giving your clients the ability to reduce risks and match people to jobs and to team leaders they will work well with could easily reduce turnover, and do so dramatically? With the right strategies, best practices, and tools, hitting these achievement goals—or even higher ones—doesn't have to be that hard.

The Human Capital Calculator report also reveals some of the best strategies and tactics for reducing labor costs. Reducing labor costs typically results from hiring people who match the demands of a job, minimizing conflict and drama between existing employees, and improving communication between team leaders and team members.

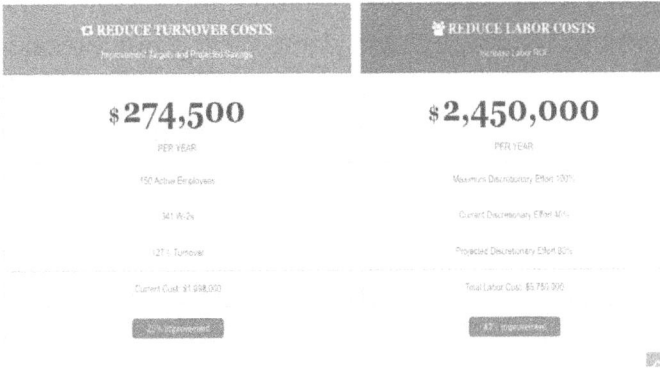

Reducing turnover costs is a big win for your clients. Improving employee engagement and reducing labor costs can be an even bigger win for your clients. Let's take a look at an example.

An easy way to reduce labor costs is to improve employee engagement, increase the discretionary effort of employees, and get more work accomplished with fewer people. When you look at employee engagement statistics, you'll find that there is a lot of room for improvement for most companies.

In a Gallup poll of 6,976 adults working for employers, it was reported that 31.5% of employees were actively engaged, enthusiastic, productive, and innovative. The same poll revealed that 52% were NOT engaged, were checked out, and were sleepwalking through the day. It also showed that 16.5% were actively DISENGAGED, destructive, disruptive, and hostile.

In the following example of a company with an annual payroll of $5,500,000, the person filling out the calculator was asked to estimate the CURRENT discretionary effort of the average employee, and using the data from the Gallup poll as a baseline, they estimated the answer was about 40%.

That meant that the company was paying for $5,500,000 worth of labor but was only getting 40% of that labor in return, which amounts to $2,200,000 worth of work.

The question was then asked, what would happen if there were ways to increase the discretionary effort of the average employee from 40% to 80%? If that could be accomplished, then the payoff would be an additional $2,200,000 per year.

As a matter of strategy, if a company has the ability to match people to their ideal jobs, then employees will be able to do what they do best and like to do most, and will accomplish MUCH more than they would if they continued sleepwalking through the day, sabotaging the company, or barely doing enough to avoid being fired.

🎖 REDUCE LABOR COSTS / INCREASE LABOR ROI

Percentage of employees:

- **Actively Engaged:** 31.5% (enthusiastic, committed, productive, innovative)
- **Not Engaged:** 52% (checked out, sleepwalk through the day)
- **Actively Disengaged:** 16.5% (destructive, disruptive, hostile)

*Estimates based Gallup polling data of 6,976 adults working for employers

Option 1. For Salaried and Hourly Employees (excluding overtime)

What is the BEST POSSIBLE EFFORT that the AVERAGE employee could contribute EACH DAY? **100%**

CURRENT Discretionary Effort Average **40%** X Annual Labor Cost **$5,500,000** = **$2,200,000**

PROJECTED Discretionary Effort Average **80%** X Annual Labor Cost **$5,500,000** = **$4,400,000**

Projected Labor Resources	- Current Labor Resources	(Additional Labor Savings/Resources Available)
$4,400,000	-$2,200,000	$2,200,000

When employees get matched to ideal supervisors, and conflicts and drama are minimized, workers can and should be much more likely to accomplish more work every day. The Human Capital Calculator shows the payoff (in dollars and cents) tied to improvements in matching applicants to jobs and the supervisors they work for.

Not only does this tool show the savings tied to reductions in employee turnover, but it also shows the savings that can be captured by improvements in employee engagement. When prospects can see real savings using their real numbers and achievable goals using time-tested tools and strategies, you will have them begging you for your help.

When people become that much more productive, we can add in the savings in overtime costs, which for this sample company is $250,000 per year. That brings the total savings tied to the improvement goals up to $2,450,000 per year.

Putting the right people in the right seats, identifying and filling performance-limiting gaps, and reducing drama and conflict in the workplace are just a few examples of additional ways you would now be able to support your clients.

The right people... in the right seats.

What problems can't be solved?

If your clients' businesses are bigger than the one we've shown in the example, their savings (or losses) would likely be much bigger numbers, but they don't have to worry about estimating, because we can plug in their EXACT numbers and provide detailed and customized reports specifically for you and your clients' companies.

Can you imagine how valuable it would be for your clients to have their own customized Human Capital Calculator analysis for each of their businesses? Suppose you entered a client's REAL numbers into the Human Capital Calculator and they realized the status quo was costing them hundreds of thousands or maybe even millions of dollars a year.

It's also reasonable to expect those losses would continue to mount year after year until something changed. So it would be like helping your clients realize they had an embezzler on their staff who was currently stealing and making more plans to continue stealing from the company, year after year, until something was done about it. If they knew they had someone embezzling that kind of money each year, how long do you think they would wait to fix it?

Remember when we told you we would teach you how to get in front of prospects when they are ready to buy? Here's how that works.

Let's pretend you were crossing the street, got hit by a bus, and were miraculously able to survive. Rest assured that the first paramedic and ambulance to arrive wouldn't have to sell you on the idea of going to the hospital.

You would be begging them to save you and hoping they could get you to the nearest hospital ASAP. You would be ready to buy their paramedic and ambulance services RIGHT THEN, and cost would not be an issue.

Well, the Human Capital Calculator has a similar effect, and prospects who didn't see a need for help before suddenly become READY TO BUY the MOMENT after the truth behind the numbers revealed in their report hits them like a bus, figuratively speaking.

And make no mistake, when you look at costs and potential savings beyond the turnover costs, as well as employee engagement, and examine the other issues addressed by the Human Capital Calculator, like employee theft, safety, and sales, the impact becomes undeniable.

Once clients see the results of the Human Capital Calculator, they must ask themselves what they're going to do about this information. And THIS is where your opportunity lies. This is where we have a system in place that can help you help your clients IDENTIFY and ADDRESS their unmet needs.

Takeaway: As we've said before, if what we've shared makes sense, then you can build a force field around your clients, get referrals without asking, and reap the long-term rewards of ongoing residual income streams for YEARS to come.

If you're like most people, you've got one big obstacle. It's resistance to change, and it's a cancer we see plaguing far too many background check companies. Of course, they don't call it cancer or even think of it as such.

The late Tom Travisano was the co-author of the book *You're Working Too Hard to Make the Sale*, and he once said something that we want to share with you. He said, "Do you know why cancer kills so many people? In far too many situations, people ignore their symptoms. They ignore the signs until the pain is so great they can't take it anymore, and when they finally do go to see a doctor, it's too late to do anything about it—or they suffer through other treatments that are far worse and more painful than was necessary. Had they just recognized and acknowledged the issues up front and taken the right steps when they should have, things might have turned out differently for many of them."

Make no mistake, your best clients are your rivals' best prospects, and they are being actively pursued. And if you aren't at least anticipating—and ideally addressing—their emerging needs, you'll have nobody else to blame WHEN, NOT IF, they go elsewhere. And, of course, it's always easier to keep an existing client than get a new one.

When it comes to revenue, and more importantly PROFIT growth, it's easy to serve existing clients with the new things they want and need because they already know, like, and trust you. When it comes to new account acquisition, it's better to be the company that clients run TO because you CAN meet their needs than it is to be the one they run FROM because you DON'T.

Chapter 4

How You (and Your Clients) Win!

What would a strategic partnership look like? What's in it for you? What's in it for your clients?

First, we want to help you build your business. That builds ours, too, and provides exceptional value to your clients, so everyone wins. We are willing to help you create white label reports for your clients that look like they came directly from you, not us, using our Human Capital Calculator FOR FREE so your clients can see—in real dollars, right now—what opportunities can be seized or lost depending on what, if anything, they choose to do differently when it comes to selecting, developing, and retaining top talent in their organizations.

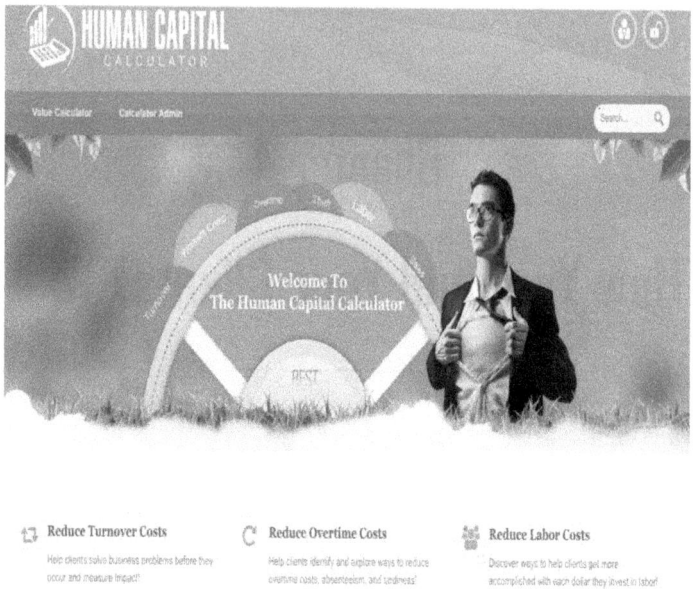

If all you did was give each of your clients a copy of their own customized Human Capital Calculator report, using their real numbers, at least you would demonstrate with your actions, and not just words, that you are proactively paying attention to your clients' needs and looking out for their best interests.

That's the kind of service that builds a FORCE FIELD around your client base and generates referrals to new clients without you having to ask. If you want to keep things real, consider this: How much would it cost to lose your best client? How about a few of your best clients? Why risk losing ANY of them when it is so easy and inexpensive to keep them?

After your clients review their report and they realize their status quo is no longer acceptable when it comes to employee retention, engagement, and performance, we have what we think (and you may agree) is a better way to help you help your clients do what Collins told people to do in his book Good to Great but didn't say how. And that is getting the right people on the bus and into the right seats. But how do you do that?

You start by finding out who is on the bus and determining what the seats look like, figuratively speaking. We suggest that businesses take inventory of their existing staff by administering a Personality Plus behavioral assessment to each and every one of their current employees, so they know who they have on their bus and what each person brings to the table.

Hiring Suite® (Web) Version 1.5

Copyright 2000-2005, Advanced Psychometrics, Inc.

EXTENDED REPORT

The electronic and/or printed booklet and this report are prepared for general use throughout the United States. Our legal counsel has advised us that all questions comply with existing Federal employment laws including the American's With Disabilities Act. However, various laws and related statutes and interpretations of them change frequently. For this reason, neither Advanced Psychometrics Incorporated nor its counsel assume responsibility for any questions included in the electronic and/or printed booklet which may violate local, state, and/or Federal laws. Users should consult their counsel about any legal concerns they may have with respect to use of these results. These results should not be construed as a recommendation to have nor hire this individual in a preemployment situation. The administrator must check previous work records, job skills required, current status, and personal references. Where safety of other workers or the public is of concern, a drug test should be administered, criminal background checks obtained, and a physical should be administered by a qualified physician. The screening mechanism utilized to produce this report does not measure political opinions or whether an individual has a tendency to commit violent acts, has any type of psychotic condition, or is sexually deviant, and can not be used for purposes of identifying political views or predicting these types of behaviors/conditions.

Name:	**PERFECT, POLLY**	Phone:	**555-555-1234**
Address:	**123 Anywhere Street**	Work Phone:	
City:	**Oshkosh**		
County:		Position:	**Secretary**
State:	**WI**	Administrator:	**Frank**
ZIP:	**75543**	Date Administered:	**5/3/2006**
		Date Graded:	**5/3/2006**

PERSONALITY PLUS®

The distortion scale deals with how candid and frank the respondent was while taking this assessment. The range for this scale is 1 to 9, with higher scores suggesting greater candor. The letter I indicates that the test is invalid due to too many unanswered questions in Section II.

The distortion score on this assessment is 7.

Organization:	10	Tension:	5
Sensitivity:	7	Probing Level:	6
Imagination:	6	Social Need:	8
Flexibility:	3	Assertive:	8
Recognition:	5	Competitive:	4

Custom profiles can be created for each position in your company by analyzing top performers. There is no additional charge for this service.

These numeric scores represent how Polly compared to **national success patterns** for each job. The closer to 100 the score, the better she fits the demands of that job.

Custom Profiles

| Sr. Prog | =85 | = | | = | | = | | = |

National Generic Patterns

Sales		Management		Office		Service		Misc	
retail	=97	warehse	=91	bookkepr	=94	hotelclk	=91	hrmgr	=94
outsales	=73	acctcomp	=97	secrtary	=100	engineer	=97	trkdrivr	=88
insales	=82	execmgmt	=82	recpntst	=97	autoserv	=91	banktell	=100
countsls	=97	salesmgr	=82	officemgr	=97	custserv	=94	apartmgr	=94
automtve	=88	financial	=97	fileclrk	=91	delivery	=91	leaseagt	=79
tellmkt	=85	techncal	=85	dataentr	=91	tchnical	=85	warehous	=91

The Personality Plus assessment was developed by Neal Johnston, a brilliant industrial psychologist, and unlike background checks and other services viewed as commodities, it is proprietary. Companies cannot get the Personality Plus except through the strategic partners whom we authorize to work with us.

By the way, we believe it is SUPER important for anyone we partner with to remain in control of THEIR client relationships. That means it is ENTIRELY up to you, and any other background check companies we partner with, to decide if your clients even know we exist behind the scenes or not.

What that means is that if we decide to work together, the companies you work with are YOUR clients and this is YOUR show. We take pride in our ability to help you serve them without interfering with what you're already doing. Here's the bottom line: If or when we ever work together, we can help you support your clients behind the scenes as much or as little as you need us to.

The TYPICAL investment for an end user or client to administer and score each Personality Plus assessment usually ranges in price, starting at $60 per person when clients invest in large quantities and going up from there. So for a company like the one in the earlier example with 150 employees, they should expect to invest about $9,000 to assess their entire staff—which, by comparison, is only about HALF of what most companies pay ONE SINGLE unskilled hourly worker over a year to mop floors, vacuum, and take out trash.

With the release of this book, we will have a special arrangement set up for you and any other strategic partners we choose to work with in the background check industry. Because behavior that is rewarded gets repeated and we know it will take bold moves to compete AND WIN against our common rivals, we're willing to make a working relationship between your company and ours WELL worth everyone's while.

In fact, if you mention our book when we speak, our company will cover the costs associated with administering the Personality Plus assessment to every current employee in each company for which you complete a Human Capital Calculator report that wants to take inventory of their existing staff using the Personality Plus.

What does that mean for you? Well, it doesn't mean you need to pass off all those savings to your clients. Feel free to charge full price or half price and keep the up-front revenue. Or if you're feeling generous, pass on the savings entirely to your clients. It's your call.

We bet you're wondering what this can look like. Well, here's an example.

Recently we were working with a company with 1,100 employees and VERY conservative improvement goals, and by using the actual numbers entered into the Human Capital Calculator directly from their payroll data, the report showed them a savings opportunity of over $9,125,353 dollars per year if they were even able to hit SOME of the lowest improvement targets they set for themselves.

The investment in assessing all their 1,100 employees at $60 each would have only been $66,000 and that was a VERY small investment compared to the ROI of over $9.1 MILLION that their own internal data suggested was not only possible but probable!

So if that had been YOUR client, you could have charged them the $66,000 and kept it all; or if you felt generous, you could have given them half off and kept $33,000 all to yourself, because we wouldn't charge you for the assessments necessary to score your client's existing staff.

Or if you REALLY wanted to build a force field around your client base, you could tell them you would cover the entire cost of their project—and watch their loyalty grow. Watch the referrals come in.

That means you could create the opportunity for SIG-NIFICANT chunks of up-front revenue for your business without having to tie up a bunch of time or other resources. Why? Because the system almost runs itself once it is set up. The time it takes to execute what we just described for a client is usually about 20 minutes total. Do that for a bunch of your clients and that could be a huge injection of up-front revenue—or the kind of good will that inspires more loyalty and referrals—with almost no extra effort.

Takeaway: You can control the amount of up-front revenue for your growing company—all that revenue for just 20 minutes of work.

Chapter 5

Tools and Training

It's vital to help clients learn what the seats on their bus look like. A custom job pattern can be created for every position in their company if they provide a list of names containing the top performers in each position.

RETAIL SALESPERSON

Area	1	2	3	4	5	6	7	8	9	10	11	12	Prof Score
A/ Organization													≈10
B/ Sensitivity													≈10
C/ Imagination													≈7
D/ Flexibility													≈10
E/ Recognition													≈10
F/ Tension													≈10
G/ Probing Level													≈10
H/ Social Need													≈10
J/ Assertive													≈10
K/ Competitive													≈10
													97

90-100 Excellent   80-89 Good   70-79 Fair   0-69 Poor

The red dots represent Polly on a scale from 1 to 12 for each trait.

The green zones represent the ideal range for each trait in each specific job position.

Regarding the "Prof Score," every time Polly fell within the green zone, she earned 10 points. Each time Polly fell outside the green zone, she earned fewer points. The farther from the green zone, the fewer points she earned.

Polly earned a total score of 97 out of 100 for RETAIL SALESPERSON.

It normally costs $500 to create a custom pattern for a position. However, if we decide to work together, we won't charge your firm to create those custom job patterns for your clients either. That doesn't mean YOU can't charge them and keep all the revenue for your firm instead.

Think about it. If you have a client company that has 7 different key positions, it would normally require an additional one-time investment of $3,500 to have all those custom patterns created. Charge whatever you want and keep it all.

If you only had 100 clients and they only wanted 5 custom patterns each, that's still an opportunity for you to earn another $250K, since 100 clients times 5 positions = 500 patterns, and 500 patterns times $500 = $250,000. Or, you could charge them nothing and generate $250K worth of good will, trust, and referrals. It can remain our little secret that we didn't charge you for any of those patterns.

Finally, we can make it possible for you to create and give each of your clients online access to an inventory management system for the employees in each of their companies. It will give them the power to match their people against their custom job patterns and get the information they need to know about what each employee needs, in VERY specific terms. It will help them get employees to perform at higher levels and stay at their company longer. One thing you might not have thought of is this: Because of the time savings it offers alone, an online inventory management system like this for their talent is easily valued at over $2,000 per year.

Let's say you get 100 clients using this system. That's another $200,000 worth of resources we can give to you to share with your clients. This power will help you strengthen your relationships, earn referrals, and deliver value that greatly exceeds what any of your clients pay for your services. Then your clients will have no reason to leave.

If you're worried that you or your clients might struggle to learn how to use all this stuff, or that you don't have the time, interest, or staff time available to explain any of this to your clients and prospects, we have you covered there, too.

We have built in step-by-step video training modules that walk clients through everything they need to know in bite-size chunks so nobody gets confused about anything. Sales, service, and training are all done FOR you! We even have a workbook for step-by-step marketing.

It's the exact same training material you and your clients would receive if you paid one of our consultants their daily consulting fees, which start at $5,000 a day plus travel expenses, to go on-site and train an executive team personally. You and your clients get unlimited access to the video training modules for FREE!

Let's face it, some big companies spend more on toilet paper for their facilities each year than it would cost to assess everyone and take inventory of their talent, build custom patterns, and utilize an inventory management system of their talent to make better decisions, faster.

Before sharing any of this with your current or future clients, it is important that you see how many tens of thousands of dollars, hundreds of thousands of dollars, or even millions of dollars your clients can recoup or capture by getting close to, hitting, or even exceeding the reasonable improvement goals they establish when they use the Human Capital Calculator.

Then we want to give you the power to share the tools, training, and technology needed to help your clients reach their goals, and do it in a way that can help you and your firm earn up-front and ongoing residual income, too.

As it relates to creating ongoing residual income streams for your business without much, if any, extra effort, we're going to let you in on a little secret. You see, we have skin in the game too, and that's why we need each other.

Why else would we provide all these amazing resources and tools for you to use in your background check business to help your clients with their existing staff issues without asking you for an arm, a leg, and your firstborn child? Beyond analyzing current employees, when your clients discover the power to find out how an APPLICANT matches (or doesn't match) each seat on their bus BEFORE they hire and invest the time and money TRAINING them, the clients also find that they have the power to solve ALL KINDS of problems BEFORE THEY EVER OCCUR.

Tony Robbins told a story in his book *Awaken the Giant Within* about a guy who was standing on the shore of a river, when along came a drowning victim screaming for help. The guy dove in, made a daring rescue, and pulled the victim to shore. Of course, he was exhausted, and as soon as he lifted his head, he noticed two more people coming downstream hollering for help. So the guy made two more daring rescues, and as he lay on the beach completely exhausted after rescuing all these people, he noticed four more people coming downstream hollering for help. The moral of the story is this: Had he just taken the time to go upriver and stop the one person throwing all these people in the river in the first place, he would have saved a lot of time and energy by dealing with the single cause of the problem upriver as opposed to the many effects downriver.

That is the beauty of pre-employment assessment. Smart employers know that if they want to reduce turnover, they must hire people who fit the job. They know that if they want to improve engagement, they also need to find ways to reduce conflict and drama. If they want to get more done, they must hire and retain people with a work ethic. If they want to increase sales, they must hire and retain people who can sell. If they want to reduce injuries, they must hire and retain people who don't abuse illegal drugs. If they want to reduce employee theft, they must hire and retain honest people.

When done correctly, employment assessment and pre-employment testing help solve those problems upriver, before they occur. When you have the tools, training, and systems to solve those kind of problems for clients and can offer them a better-than-money-back guarantee that does more than just eliminate their risk, you and your business become a Purple Cow and are NOT like all the other background check companies out there.

If you want to remain a brown cow and keep doing what you've always done, we wish you the best but are not really that interested in working with you, and it would probably be a waste of time to engage in a conversation past this.

If this does makes sense to you, we want you to earn your clients' pre-employment testing business in the future, and we are confident you will once you and your clients implement the tools and training we have put into place to make things better within their existing staff. The ongoing residual revenue streams tied to pre-employment assessment are just another reason we think smart background check companies will want to add assessments to their offerings.

It's a new and different way for you to help your clients reduce their risk. The margins are higher, and your prospects and customers can't just get these products anywhere. And since we are willing to provide FUTURE pre-employment assessments at wholesale prices to the background check companies we choose to form strategic partnerships with, this creates a win-win-win scenario where our firm makes money providing assessments to you at wholesale prices.

Your firm makes money providing assessments to your prospects and clients at retail prices. And your current and future clients capture savings and revenue dealing with both current challenges and the future issues "upriver" that they wouldn't have otherwise.

Since change is a constant when it comes to employment because of growth, retirements, and promotions, putting an employee assessment and pre-employment testing system in place at your client locations is like installing a toll both in their HR office that pays you every time applicants walk through their doors.

If you are already offering background checks, it's like you already have toll booths in place; the difference is that you would just make a LOT more money on every car that comes through your toll both. Plus, by working with us, you will attract more cars than you could by offering background checks alone.

And once you see the margins, we're sure you'll agree that the PROFIT is much higher on assessment tools than it is on background checks—but this isn't an either-or choice. You can offer both. We think you SHOULD offer both, and we think your clients will be better off because of it. Think about more cars, more revenue per car, and more profit per car.

Think about that. Let it sink in.

Takeaway: What all this means to you as a strategic partner is that there will be a continual demand and ANOTHER ongoing stream of passive residual income for you and us. It's a win-win for everyone involved. The cost savings and revenue opportunities you AND your clients capture by working with us that you wouldn't have otherwise make this partnership a no-brainer, especially since any investments your clients make in pre-employment assessment services should amount to nothing more than a small fraction of the savings we worked together to help them capture. So we are really just offering you and your clients a better way to do business that pays for itself multiple times over when implemented properly.

If you feel good about what you've read, it sounds like it makes sense, and you'd like to look a little deeper, then we invite you to go to our website (see below) and click on the link where it says "How to Become a Strategic Partner - Click Here" so we can learn a little about you and your firm, too, before we visit.

https://amohumancapital.com/

Chapter 6

The Wrap-Up

f it makes sense to you to work with us, here is a list and summary of what we can do to help and support you and your business.

For our background check strategic partners whom we elect to work with, we will do several things:

- **First,** we will give you the ability to run Human Capital Calculator reports for your clients. Are you worried you won't know what to say or how to present the reports?

  o Don't worry—we have step-by-step guides to walk you through everything you need to say and do to best serve your clients and position yourself as an expert.

  o If you ever did color-by-number pictures when you were a kid, it's kind of like that, but instead of creating a picture, we are creating a sense of urgency that will make your clients want to do more business with you right now without taking up a bunch of your time.

- **Second,** we will give you the ability to use our proprietary online systems to easily help your clients take inventory of the strengths and opportunities for improvement within their existing staff at no charge. You, of course, can use our products and charge as much as you see fit, and keep all associated fees.

- **Third,** you will have the power to help clients identify who is on their bus using the Personality Plus behavioral assessment and identify what each seat on their bus looks like by creating custom job patterns based on their top performers in each of those positions.

- **Fourth,** you will be granted the power to give clients access to an inventory management system for their people online that can help them improve engagement, performance, and retention of their existing employees AND make better hiring decisions in the future so they can do it right the first time instead of doing it over. When that happens, you end up with a force field around your client base, and you create up-front and ongoing revenue streams from pre-employment assessments that require little or no extra effort—because the clients and the systems we've built do almost all of the work for you. When you help clients avoid costs and hassles that are exponentially greater than what your professional services cost, it shouldn't be a surprise when they go out of their way to tell others and you get phone calls from prospects you've never met begging you to help their businesses too.

- **Fifth,** you will receive access to "done-for-you" training and marketing resources.

  - o Don't have the time or interest in explaining these tools and how to use them to clients? No problem. We have a modular video-based training system that does all that work for you.

  - o Don't want to make sales presentations? It's not a problem. It has been our experience that when someone sees the results of their Human Capital Calculator report, they will be begging you for help anyway.

  - o For prospects who haven't been exposed to the Human Capital Calculator, we made a video that explains everything for you without referencing our company name or contact information so you can use it as your own on your website, social media, or email marketing. When we say we have done-for-you marketing in place and ready to go, we mean it.

Icing on the cake: As for best practices, if that's not enough, we offer a better-than-money-back guarantee that eliminates the entire financial risk for end users and our strategic partners who work with them on every project, so there is never anything to have to apologize for or defend. It's a win for your clients. It's a win for you and your firm. It's a win for us. And that's the way it should be.

This isn't something that takes days, weeks, months, or years to pull off. We've already invested the time and spent the money necessary to condense and streamline everything to the essentials.

We feel confident, given all the support mechanisms in place, that we've streamlined things so you can be ready to start helping your clients in a single afternoon. And finally, obviously, it's only fair for all involved that our partners share a significant portion of the ongoing pre-employment assessment revenue while we work behind the scenes to provide support.

The good news is that we aren't stingy, and we think you'll find the profit margin on our products to be quite rewarding if we ever get the chance to discuss those numbers.

Imagine what you could do with a BUNCH of new clients! And because our company and platform can support as many new clients as you can add—without you having to add headcount, buy more equipment, or add office space to keep up with your growth—that's just more revenue you can use however you want.

The only thing you'd have to decide then is what to do with the extra revenue. Would you use the extra revenue to hire more people to support the other aspects of your business that are labor-intensive, so you can have more free time or do other things you are passionate about, like spend time with your family or go on vacations? Would you just put it in the bank and take pleasure in watching your account grow? Would you like to make your business more valuable to turn over to your kids someday?

Would you want to be able to command a higher selling price and make your business more attractive to potential buyers? Whatever you decide, it's entirely up to you.

In closing, we need to warn you and make something crystal clear:

This isn't one of those get-rich-quick schemes that promises you fame and fortune for doing nothing. That's not our style and it's not what we're about.

So here's the scoop. The system we've put together isn't pie-in-the-sky, ivory tower stuff. It's a sensible, prudent, and fundamentally sound strategy supported with step-by-step instruction and all the tools needed to implement it.

In no way are we suggesting or promising that everyone (or anyone) who partners with us is going to make any amount of money. Who knows, you might not even care about making more money because you're making enough already, and you just want to take great care of your clients and solidify—or even expand—your reputation as THE thought leader in your market. And that's OK too. We get it.

That's just our way of saying that we don't have any idea how much you or anyone else who partners with us will make, and that's why we think of it as more of a pilot program. We certainly have goals and believe they can be achieved—otherwise we wouldn't have put all this together.

We are certain little or nothing will change for you, or us, if you become a strategic partner and don't take action and follow the steps and use the tools correctly, but that's pretty much true of anything that's worth-while.

This isn't like any business-building system for back-ground check providers you've ever seen. There's no fluff or filler—just battle-tested strategies, tactics, and tools that have been adapted SPECIFICALLY for your industry.

And it's easy to understand. You can get through it in an afternoon. It's about MORE than just consulting, too. It's easy!

As part of the program, our goals are to collect and analyze feedback from established and growth-ori-ented background check companies looking to add a minimum of $200,000 to $2.5 million a year in extra profit, and we believe it can be done without adding headcount or detracting from your current efforts. If working with us can't result in you increasing PROFITS by $200,000 at a bare minimum for a small firm, and ideally closer to $2.5 million or more per year for a mid-size or larger firm, then we doubt our goals are closely aligned—and that's OK. Even though that means it probably isn't the right time for us to work to-gether, we're glad we were able to share information.

As a bonus, you will have access to our knowledgea-ble team, who will personally guide you step by step through the process. We want every person and company we work with to walk away glad that they know us and feeling like they are better off because they do.

Takeaway: You have nothing to lose and lots to gain. The same goes for your clients. The next step is up to you. Go to our site, click on the link, and answer the questions. We look forward to learning about you and your firm and visiting with you soon. Don't delay. Waiting one day, or one week, might be all the time that is necessary for someone else to slide in and grab the last of the remaining spots in our pilot program. We don't want to be the one who must give you that bad news or put you on a waiting list.

An old mentor once said that indecision is a decision, and the only things that come to those who wait are the leftovers from the people who hustle. He was right.

How does a background check and employment screening company become a strategic partner and qualify for wholesale pricing, support, and training on the assessment products and services?

Click on the link labeled "How to Become a Strategic Partner" at https://amohumancapital.com/ and answer the questions on the short questionnaire that is presented. We will follow up with you once your information has been reviewed.

Chapter 7

The Workbook

Section 1

How to Grow Your Background Screening Business

Repeat the steps listed below every month. Engage clients. Build curiosity. Earn more revenue.

Week 1

- Make an announcement – via email, social media, print, dashboards.

Week 2

- Post/send out the intro videos listed on the admin links page.

Week 3

- Pick a social media video to send out with a "how we can help" update.

Section 2

Important Administrative Links

In this section you will find video links explaining in detail the BENEFITS for your company, as well as explaining "reverse risk" to your clients. These are easy-to-use "on-demand" tools built in to simplify communication with your team and your clients.

Promotional Option A

- Use this video link to provide a quick explanation to <u>clients</u>: https://vimeo.com/323866831

- Use this video link to provide more in-depth information to your <u>clients</u>: <u>https://vimeo.com/267714802</u>

- Use this FREE download link to get the PDF of Mason Duchatschek's book *People Matter Most*: <u>https://drive.google.com/file/d/1Z2is-JhSjpIKZjh5WwajwO2Is9RWZo-EYN/view?usp=sharing</u>

Promotional Option B

Want to know how to sell background checks, drug tests, and employment tests to more prospects and clients (so you can increase sales revenue, attract more clients, and increase profits) WITHOUT HAVING TO SELL?

Step 1: Show the video linked below to your clients and prospects. (It has no reference to any other company, phone number, or website, so you can use this promotional video as your own.)

https://vimeo.com/395548051

Step 2: Ask your prospect/client if there is any step they are willing to risk skipping to save a few bucks.

Step 3: When they say "no," it means they want to buy drug tests, background checks, and employment tests from you (or someone else if you don't offer all these services). So all you have to do is help them get started.

Section 3

Tweets for Twitter / Short Facebook Updates

In this section you will find quick video links offering short, engaging tweets or posts to get the attention of your followers. Using these short posts every 3–4 days will continue to build your online presence and create curiosity.

How can we help you reduce turnover?
https://vimeo.com/331266158

How can we help you reduce workers' comp costs?
https://vimeo.com/331264502

How can we help you reduce employee theft?
https://vimeo.com/331272218

How can we help you increase sales and retain customers? https://vimeo.com/331274423

Want to increase the ROI of your employee engagement efforts? https://vimeo.com/331268682

What are our customers saying?
https://vimeo.com/218837332

Section 4

Letter Content / Website Announcements (Email, Print, Facebook & Blogs)

These are ready-to-use marketing messages you can put to use right away. Remember to utilize any and all forms of communication you may have with your clients—dashboards, emails, Facebook direct messages, inserts in mailed invoices, etc. Let people know you are here to be their one-stop shop.

Don't forget to utilize <u>any and all forms of communication!</u>

Announcement #1

<u>Subject:</u>

Announcement: A negotiation on your behalf ...

<u>Message:</u>

Great news! We've discovered a new way to help clients that is so valuable it may very well exceed the investment you make in our services each year—many times over.

Contact us today if you or your organization is struggling with any of the following challenges:

1) Increasing sales, productivity, or client retention

2) Reducing employee turnover

3) Minimizing employee conflict and drama

Announcement #2

Subject:

Got sandbaggers?

Message:

I'm not talking about people literally filling sandbags, like if there was a flood or something. I'm talking about employees doing just enough work not to get fired. You know the type.

I'm not saying it's OK, but I understand why this happens, and it could be costing you a FORTUNE. (Hint: It might even be YOUR fault.)

Never fear. We've discovered a new way to help clients with this problem.

If this is an issue in your company, reach out to your customer service representative to find out how to **solve this problem** now and help **prevent it** from happening in the future!

Announcement #3:

<u>Subject:</u>

Customer service training to fix hiring mistakes

<u>Message:</u>

For the sake of discussion, let's say that two new hires go through the exact same customer service training program and learn what to say to difficult customers in different situations.

Unfortunately, HOW they talk to customers can be MORE important than what they say.

Can they take the pressure and work with customers who push their buttons?

What good is customer service training if your reps do what they are supposed to do, but in a way that makes things worse instead of better?

Want to find out which of your employees **have what it takes** BEFORE you put them in positions they aren't cut out for?

If so, reach out to your customer service representative to find out how to **solve this problem** now and help **prevent it** from happening in the future!

Announcement #4:

Subject:

Fun & Games (until someone gets hurt & YOU have to pay for it)

Message:

What if accidents were as easy to prevent as keeping fire away from gasoline? Well, they are. (Hint: It's not always about safety training.)

Sometimes accident prevention is as simple as making sure good workers don't make bad decisions and show up for work under the influence of drugs or alcohol.

Other times it can be as simple as making sure you put people with calm, organized, and compliant personalities in certain work environments instead of people without these traits.

If you want the power to know how to match people and their personalities with the jobs you have so you can avoid unnecessary injuries, conflicts, and sub-par performance, then I encourage you to **reach out to your customer service representative** and get access to some new resources we've acquired that can help resolve and prevent these issues.

Announcement #5:

<u>Subject:</u>

How growing people is like planting a garden

<u>Message:</u>

Do you treat your employees like a garden that is your only source of food?

An "old-school" IBM sales manager named John Hauser once asked same that question. Then he said, "Growing people is like planting a garden. Start with quality seeds, provide them with nourishment, and give them time to grow."

Think about it. Do you treat the people in your organization like you would a garden that you depended on for your ONLY nourishment and growth?

If not, do you want to know how to do this? Reach out to us today to find out how to **solve this problem** now and help **prevent it** from happening in the future!

Section 5

The Assessment Education Series

In this section we have ready-to-use training videos and tools available to ensure that end users are properly trained in implementing and understanding assessments. It is required that the leadership—most typically someone in a human resources role—take the education series and pass a quick test at the end.

P.S. We've included the length of each video so you can plan accordingly!

Introduction (Watch this first.)

Employee Selection Secrets: Strategy and Tactics (11:08)

http://vimeo.com/buildatribe/review/117628859/084d8279dd

Assessment Basics

The Johnston Index Basic Skills Assessment (2:57)

http://vimeo.com/buildatribe/review/117295119/411e9d0fbd

The Insure Survey - The Secrets of Hiring Honest, Reliable Employees With a Work Ethic (8:29) http://vimeo.com/buildatribe/re-view/117295117/c1376af480

The Personality Plus - Training Video #1 (8:36)

http://vimeo.com/buildatribe/re-view/117295125/1be212a50a

The Personality Plus - Training Video #2 (8:23)

http://vimeo.com/buildatribe/re-view/117628858/5966689eac

Team Master - How to Minimize Conflict, Improve Performance and Reduce Risk of Lawsuits (8:33)

http://vimeo.com/buildatribe/re-view/117295139/88b62cc4eb

Strategy and Tactics

A Way to Introduce the Selection Process to Appli-cants and Get Them to Reveal Info They Might Have Tried to Hide (2:49)

http://vimeo.com/buildatribe/re-view/117291866/875f7e589b

The Hiring Funnel - Sample Selection Processes for Hourly and Salaried Employees (3:56)

http://vimeo.com/buildatribe/re-view/117376943/12a9caf9e6

Imprinting - A Secret to Improved New Employee Retention and Performance (5:18)

http://vimeo.com/buildatribe/review/117317494/3b6364fbb6

Inventory of Talent - How to Manage Your Inventory of Talent (5:29)

http://vimeo.com/buildatribe/review/117291864/6a8096c25c

Site Functionality/Navigation

Site Tour - Explore the Functionality of Your Scoring Site (11:41)

http://vimeo.com/buildatribe/review/117291865/2e73d0caf1

Multi-location Systems - How to Transfer Units and Create Team Master Reports (3:08)

http://vimeo.com/buildatribe/review/117608801/51d74ffde4

How to Create a Team Master Report (1:54)

http://vimeo.com/buildatribe/review/117317498/5c6a90be0a

Frequently Asked Questions

Q&A - Frequently Asked Questions (11:47)

http://vimeo.com/buildatribe/review/117317497/eb2c687b49

<u>Section 6</u>

Frequently Asked Questions

1. What do clients get?

They receive:

a. Their own web-based inventory management system for their talent (aka The Hiring Suite)

b. The Personality Plus behavioral assessment for each of their current employees (regularly $60 per employee)

c. Access to Mason Duchatschek's "Assessment Education Series," which is a modular online video training system that describes how to maximize the power of the assessments and the inventory management system of talent

d. Creation of custom "success patterns" when significant numbers of top performers are identified by the client and available for any given position

2. What's the "better-than-money-back" guarantee?

Once all employees have been assessed using the Personality Plus, within the next 30 days, if a client doesn't feel their investment was worth exponentially more than they invested, they may receive a 100%

money-back guarantee and they may keep all the as-sessments of their existing staff, access to training vid-eos, and use of the Hiring Suite online system. The only requirement is that key executives complete the training modules and pass the "certification test" with a score of 80% or better. (It is a 30-question true-or-false test.)

The video at this link explains it in further detail: https://vimeo.com/267714802

3. Are there any additional costs or obligations re-quired of your clients or participants?

No. The focus of this project is entirely on the assess-ment, development, and management of EXISTING employees in your clients' companies, and the fees for these services have been covered as part of this pro-gram.

However, if your clients wish to acquire additional as-sessments in the future to assess potential job appli-cants (as part of a pre-employment testing program), then they will have the option to purchase them at that time if they choose. There is NO OBLIGATION TO PURCHASE ASSESSMENTS OF ANY KIND AT ANY TIME.

4. Can your clients have their current employees assessed with the Personality Plus a few at a time or as often as they choose?

No. The assessment of current employees is a one-time offer. As part of this initiative, a client company may receive a Personality Plus assessment (regularly $60 each) for each of the full-time and part-time employees who are on their payroll and have them complete the assessment questionnaire by the assessment scoring date/deadline. The assessment scoring date/deadline is the date the client company specifies as the date by which all current employees must have completed their Personality Plus questionnaire.

5. Can a client request individual assessment results before the results are available for all the rest of the current employees?

No. When the assessment scoring date/deadline has passed, all current employees who have completed the Personality Plus questionnaire will have their assessments scored together, in one batch.

6. If a few current employees fail to complete their Personality Plus questionnaire before the assessment scoring date, will their results be included in the client company's data at a later date?

No and yes (it depends). Once the assessment scoring date/deadline has passed, every employee who has completed the Personality Plus questionnaire will be scored, and their data will be transferred into the client's inventory management system for their talent (aka the Hiring Suite scoring site). So in this case, the answer is no.

However, after the assessment scoring date/deadline has passed, any current employees who failed to complete their questionnaire on time will always have the option of *taking it again at the client's expense*. So in this case the answer is yes, IF the late individuals are willing to retake the questionnaire and the member is willing to pay for each additional assessment.

7. What if a current employee tries to "fake" their results on the Personality Plus or doesn't take it seriously and checks random boxes? Can clients have them take it again, and have the costs covered, too?

This does happen. When it does, it triggers low scores on what is known as the "distortion scale," and this topic is covered in detail in the training videos. If the individual who did this is willing to retake the questionnaire and the client is willing to pay for each additional assessment, then the results can be added to the client's inventory management system for their talent (aka the Hiring Suite scoring site). The costs of having individual employees retake the Personality Plus are NOT covered.

8. Several other assessments are mentioned in the Assessment Education Series, like the Johnston Index (basic skills assessment) and the Insure Survey (measuring integrity, substance abuse, reliability, and work ethic). Are the costs of those assessments included for clients' existing employees too?

Those two assessments are discussed in the Assessment Education Series and are geared toward pre-employment testing purposes. They are also integrated into the Hiring Suite online system. Because each client's initial project is focused on helping them with issues related to current employees, the Johnston Index and Insure Survey are not administered as part of this process.

The Johnston Index and Insure Survey are available to clients who have completed the Assessment Education Series and want to purchase them for pre-employment testing of job applicants in the future.

However, Team Master reports (which are also derived from Personality Plus questionnaire data) ARE available at no additional charge for current employees who completed the Personality Plus questionnaire before the assessment scoring date/deadline.

9. What is the process like?

We take inventory of strengths and weaknesses for each of your client's employees by identifying their suitability to perform different jobs within the company. Inventory is taken by administering a powerful and incredibly thorough behavioral assessment to each employee (the Personality Plus).

We give your clients the option to list key positions in their company and identify the top performers in each of them. For each position where at least 10-15 top performers have been identified, we will compile the statistical data from the top performers that were specified and create a "custom success pattern" to be loaded onto an electronic database/inventory management system of talent (aka the Hiring Suite). For positions where fewer than 10-15 top performers can be designated, an alternative data-gathering method will be used.

This system can then be used to aid in future decisions regarding employee development, management, and promotions as well as decisions regarding hiring.

Think of it as a web-based inventory management system for human resources.

The Assessment Education Series is a web-based video training series provided for all your clients.

10. How does a background check company become a strategic partner and qualify for wholesale pricing, support, and training on the assessment products and services?

Click on the link labeled "How to Become a Strategic Partner" at https://amohumancapital.com/ and answer the questions on the short questionnaire that is presented. We will follow up with you once your information has been reviewed.

Bonus Chapter

Workplace Drug Testing and the One-Stop Shop Concept

After all these years in business, there is one thing that continues to surprise us. It is the failure of smart and experienced business owners and executives to grasp one simple truth: that it is RE-ALLY expensive to be cheap. You probably see it all the time—some clients will drop you in a heartbeat if they think they can save a nickel, even if your service is great.

Once upon a time, Mason decided he wanted to get in shape and compete in a triathlon. He hadn't ridden a bike since he was a kid, and since a triathlon consists of a swim, bike, and run, he needed to buy a bike.

He could have gotten a brand-new bike from Walmart for about $100-$200. He also had the choice of spending $1,000–$2,000 to get a new bike from a professional bike shop.

In the end, he spent 10 times more than he would have spent at Walmart because Ed Foster, the owner of Sunset Cyclery in St. Louis, Missouri, asked him a few important questions.

He asked how many miles a week Mason would be training for his race. He asked how many months he would be training. He asked how long Mason's rides would be, and where he planned on doing his training.

When Mason told him he would be riding over 100–150 miles a week for several months leading up to the race, Ed asked a few more relevant questions. He said, "Mason, when you are 30 miles from home and the cheap bike you bought at Walmart breaks down and leaves you stranded in the middle of nowhere, will you feel good about the fact you spent less on a cheap bike?

"If you go flying down a hill at 42 mph and the bike that was put together by a kid being paid a little over minimum wage falls apart the first time you hit a bump at high speed, and you wake up in the hospital, will you feel good about the fact you spent less to get a cheap bike?"

Needless to say, Mason bought the expensive bike. And he was SO happy he did.

What does that story have to do with business? Everything.

We want to share with you a simple strategy that we share with our end users/clients. It's a step-by-step treasure map explaining exactly how to implement this one strategy that can help clients overcome some of their businesses' biggest obstacles and solve a whole bunch of their other business problems before they occur.

Think of it like bowling—rolling one ball down the alley and then knocking down lots of pins all in one swoop. Well, this strategy works kind of like that. It's one strategy, but it helps clients eliminate lots of business problems (instead of pins), and they can do it all in one swoop.

The strategy we're going to share is related to employee selection secrets and best practices.

If clients want to increase sales, they should hire and retain people who can sell.

If clients want to reduce absenteeism and tardiness, they should hire and retain people who are reliable.

If clients want to get more work accomplished with fewer people and minimize overtime costs, they should hire and retain people who have a work ethic.

If clients want to reduce turnover, they should hire and retain people who have the skill, attitude, and personality required to match the demands of a job.

If clients want to minimize accidents in the workplace, then they should hire and retain drug-free employees.

If clients want to reduce employee theft, time theft, or fraudulent workers' comp, they should hire and retain employees with integrity who won't steal or fake injuries.

If clients want to prevent negligent hiring lawsuits, they should avoid applicants with a history and track record of problems.

Wouldn't you agree that the people you hire either solve business problems or create new ones? It's pretty much true everywhere, isn't it?

You can let your clients waste years of hard work and thousands of dollars to learn what we're about to share, or you can just follow the step-by-step blueprints we are about to lay out for you.

In this example, we will show you a best-practices employee selection process that was designed to help employers gather as much accurate job-related information as they possibly can, as quickly as possible, and without putting an unnecessary strain on their resources.

Failure to gather as much job-related information as employers possibly can about every single applicant before making an offer is like agreeing to play Russian roulette without first checking every chamber to make sure it is clear.

There is a logical flow to the process highlighted in the funnel we're about to share with you. You will notice that the process treats all applicants fairly and consistently. You will also notice that each person who makes it through the entire process will have been thoroughly screened using applications, background checks, drug tests, and interviews, as well as skill-, attitude-, and personality-based assessment tools.

For a salaried or professional position, the funnel looks like this.

Sample Selection Process Funnel: Salaried / Professional Positions

Pre-Hire

1. Accept Application/Resume

2. Administer Johnston Index, Insure, Personality Plus

3. Review Application / Resume

4. Score and Review Johnston Index Results

5. Score and Review Insure Survey Results

6. Initial Phone Screen and/or Interview

7. Score and Review Personality Plus Results

8. Conduct Final Interviews

9. Background Checks/Reference Checks/Drug Tests

10. Trial Period / Probation

Post Hire

Orientation (Print Team Master Report and Personality Plus Results for Orientation/Imprinting Session)

Step 1 is to accept applications and/or resumes.

Step 2 is to administer three different pre-employment assessments that are meant to evaluate the job match in terms of skills, attitudes, and behaviors required by the job. The Johnston Index is a basic skills assessment that measures problem-solving, math, vocabulary, and spelling skills. The Insure Survey measures integrity, reliability, work ethic, and attitudes toward substance abuse. The Personality Plus measures 10 different behavioral traits that employers can use to match a person to the demands of the job.

Step 3 is to review the applications and resumes. Those lacking the desired qualifications are tossed out of the funnel and do not continue in the selection process.

Step 4 is to score and review the results of the Johnston Index assessment. Those applicants lacking basic skills are removed from the funnel and do not continue in the selection process.

Step 5 is to score and review the results of the Insure Survey. Applicants clearly lacking in integrity, reliability, work ethic, or desired attitudes toward substance abuse are eliminated from the funnel.

Step 6 is to conduct an initial phone screen and/or interview.

Step 7 is to score and review the Personality Plus results to make sure the behaviors required by the job match the person. For example, if someone is an introvert, a job like being a Walmart greeter might not be a good fit. Or if a person is very sensitive, a job in collections, customer service, or sales, where they are likely to experience rudeness, angry clients, and outright rejection, could seem like torture.

Step 8 is to conduct final interviews.

Step 9 is to conduct background checks, reference checks, and drug tests to minimize other work-related risks as well as the possibility of ending up on the wrong end of a negligent hiring lawsuit (where your company could be held liable for criminal or torturous acts conducted by employees toward co-workers or customers).

Step 10 is a trial period, which gives employers the ability to "test drive" new workers before they become full-time employees.

At the top of the funnel, there are more applicants, and the steps near the top are fast, easy, and inexpensive to implement. As employers get further down in the funnel, the time and investment made in evaluating remaining applicants increases while the number of applicants who make it to each new step decreases.

The people who make it to the bottom of the funnel have been thoroughly screened; employers have done their jobs properly and maximized the probability of getting the best people. They've also minimized the probability of getting the worst.

Like we said earlier, it is REALLY expensive to be cheap when it comes to business, and as it relates to hiring, the rewards tied to good decisions and the consequences tied to bad decisions couldn't be farther apart.

What's the difference between what a top salesperson sells in a year and what the worst salesperson sells? How many times can an employer afford to pick the wrong one?

Of course employers could save a few bucks by skipping the Insure Survey in their process. But will they feel good about that decision when they have people embezzling money or faking injuries? Will they be OK with paying unnecessary overtime costs because they have unreliable people skipping work and/or showing up late?

Of course employers could save a few bucks by skipping the Personality Plus. As Mason's mom says, "If you don't take the time to do something right the first time, you'll have to make time to do it over." And will employers feel good if they have to keep replacing the people who don't fit, over and over, when they could have known ahead of time that applicants weren't going to work out?

Of course employers could skip drug tests and background checks and save a few dollars there as well. But will they feel good about that decision when they find themselves in a lawsuit with no defense because they were, in fact, negligent and cut a few corners to save a few dollars?

We shared this funnel so employers know how to cover all the bases. They can take our word for it or find out the hard way.

Mason had a client one time who had a funnel similar to this for their warehouse workers in a large retail sporting goods chain. At some point, the client felt they didn't have an employee theft problem and could save a few dollars by cutting the assessments measuring integrity from their process. It didn't take long before they noticed things like expensive baseball gloves, bats, and high-end sunglasses going missing—lots of them. Then they had to buy more security cameras, hire loss-prevention specialists, and eventually hire lawyers to press charges.

Dr. Greg Lousig-Nont, an industrial psychologist in Las Vegas, used to say that you can't judge a crook by their cover. He was right, and that retail sporting goods chain learned that lesson the hard way.

We aren't saying that employers can't hire good people if they skip any of the steps in the process we've laid out. They might get lucky more often than not, but luck isn't a strategy, and why risk it if they don't have to.

So are we suggesting to business owners in the background check industry that you should add pre-employment testing AND drug testing to your offerings? The answer is YES.

When one of your clients or prospects watches this video (https://vimeo.com/395548051) and they realize they should be using ALL of those tools and services to protect themselves, do you really want to have to send them ELSEWHERE when they could be getting ALL those services from you?

If you aren't offering pre-employment assessments, click on the link labeled "How to Become a Strategic Partner" at https://amohumancapital.com/ and answer the questions on the short questionnaire that is presented. We will follow up with you once your information has been reviewed.

If you aren't offering drug testing services yet and you know you should be, then we invite you to reach out to Tyler Weston at Noble Diagnostics (tyler@noblediagnostics.com / 262-957-1968 / www.NobleDiagnostics.com) and inquire about their strategic partner program designed especially for people in the background check business. The leadership team at Noble Diagnostics can set you up with wholesale pricing, world-class support, and expert training as well.

Their story began in 1998, when company founder Dan Hlavachek was an early adopter and pioneer in emerging drug testing technologies—now referred to as on-site drug testing and rapid testing kits. These kits offered lab-quality accuracy and results in minutes (instead of hours or days) at a fraction of the cost of industry norms. Their main market was healthcare and occupational health centers all over the United States, Africa, Europe, Mexico, South America, and Australia.

By 2003, Dan saw (and later seized) opportunities to create and provide third-party drug and alcohol testing program administration services to businesses of all kinds. He and his team set up networks of trained drug and alcohol testing administrators, collection sites, and laboratories all over the country. Once this was completed, they offered a full-service menu of both substance abuse testing AND program administration services. They are now opening their network and back-end support systems to background check and assessment service providers looking to expand their business and better serve the needs of their clients.

Back in the day, clients were farming out their business related to background checks to background check companies, drug tests to drug testing companies, and employment testing to employment testing companies. The risk-mitigation industry had different silos. It was (and still is) cumbersome for customers who utilize multiple vendors, and it doesn't need to be that way when the alternative for packaged offerings exists.

Your best clients are your competitors' best prospects. The modern workplace is defined by numerous risks. There are products, services, and strategies that help employers minimize those risks, and if you don't offer them to the prospects and clients who need them, someone else will.

Customers understand and value simplicity. They like and appreciate bundled service offerings. They like getting one invoice instead of many. If they already like and trust you, why force them to go looking elsewhere?

As with the background check industry, there are tons of regulations that govern the drug and alcohol testing industry. In fact, it can seem overwhelming, and that's why it is important to partner with experienced and battle-tested drug testing industry leaders who know the ropes and can help you avoid unnecessary pitfalls.

Chances are, you've already mastered the background check portion of your business. There is no need to reinvent the wheel and learn the assessment industry or drug and alcohol testing industry from scratch.

To maintain your brand image, the assessments as well as the substance abuse offerings can be custom-labeled so the products and services look like they are coming directly from you! Because of their high-volume buying power, the team at Noble Diagnostics can give you access to products and services at excellent margins, which means exceptional profit opportunities for the strategic partners that work with them.

Expert training is provided. Support is in place. And you can focus on what matters most: the relationship between you and your clients and your future clients.

The Big Takeaway

Want to know how to sell background checks, drug tests, and employment tests to more prospects and clients (so you can increase sales revenue, attract more clients, and increase profits) WITHOUT HAVING TO SELL?

Step 1: Show the following video to your clients and prospects. (It has no reference to any other company, phone number, or website, so you can use this promotional video as your own.)

https://vimeo.com/395548051

Step 2: Ask your prospect/client if there is any step they are willing to risk skipping to save a few bucks.

Step 3: When they say "no," it means they want to buy drug tests, background checks, and employment tests from you (or someone else, if you don't offer all these services). So all you have to do is help them get started.